AF427038

IT BEGINS WITH A BOOK

An Everyday Guide to Growing Young Readers

Christy Smith

It Begins with a Book: An Everyday Guide to Growing Young Readers

@2025 Christy Smith

All rights reserved. No portion of this book may be reproduced in any form without the prior written permission of the publisher.

Published in Orange County, California, by It Begins with a Book Publishing.

ISBN 979-8-218-60469-1

Printed in the United States of America

Cover image: Steve Bjorkman

To my family and friends, thank you for sharing
your love of reading. And to families and children
everywhere, may you always find joy in books, and may
the gift of reading inspire you to share with others.

TABLE OF CONTENTS

Dear Reader:

Congrats! You have taken the first and possibly most important step toward creating a lifelong reader. You have picked up this book to discover something magical, because the secret to instilling a love of reading in your child—well, it begins with a book!

Growing little readers might feel like a daunting task. You might not know where to start, you might not love reading, life is busy, and you need more time. These are valid thoughts. However, I'm here to tell you it can be easy, inexpensive, and manageable for your busy schedule. In less time than your daily social media scroll and for less than your latte and lemon loaf, you can invest your valued time and money into setting fabulous foundations for literacy.

Here's what this book will do for you:

- Equip you with hands-on information in short chapters with practical, easy-to-implement suggestions for at-home reading.

- Provide background information regarding why, what, when, and how to read to your little ones.

- Encourage creative literacy with ways to implement FUN in the stories, books, and literature you explore daily.

- Offer a one-sentence takeaway at the end of each chapter—a quick way to see how you can "grow" your little reader.

Designed with four distinct sections, *It Begins with a Book* will guide you through the ages and stages of young readers.

Get started early and begin reading at birth! This section highlights some research and recommendations to prepare our homes for our littlest readers. We will explore what, when, and how to introduce books to little ones, along with suggestions for building a home library.

Read, read, read! As we embark on the joyful reading journey for our kids, we benefit from tips and tools to help us. This section will dive into book experiences and ways to involve our littles in literature. And the best way to do that is to read, read, read!

Optimize opportunities as we celebrate reading milestones and independence while remaining connected to the literature our children engage with in their newfound literacy. Creative invitations to explore literature in new ways will help keep reading routines interesting and exciting. We want to optimize our opportunities!

Wonder, whimsy, wishes! When we find wonder and whimsy in our world, we can create moments that extend the literature our littles read. Let's get creative and make reading fun! This section showcases ideas we can implement to enhance book experiences with our families. Here, we can take the wishes of our dandelion dreams and turn them into literacy legacies!

I'm thrilled you've joined me on this journey, and I'm proud of you for starting today. Each time you open a book with your little one, you are taking one step toward setting a firm foundation in literacy. You've got this, and I'm cheering for you! So, now, let's get to the good stuff!

Joyfully,
Christy

WHY THIS BOOK, WHY NOW?

It Begins with a Book is a practical guide for parents, grand-parents, homeschoolers, caregivers, and those leading the littlest learners. The carefully designed chapters are short and packed with tidbits that families can easily apply. This hands-on guide clearly emphasizes why we read, what to read, and how to implement creative literacy at home to encourage our young ones to become lifelong readers.

It Begins with a Book was born from my deep desire for each child to have an opportunity to love reading. As a former elementary teacher with twenty-three years of experience, I spent my career teaching reading. It was my passion, and I pursued advanced literacy education to support each reader in my classroom. My heart for students became a driving force for my learning and growth. I saw firsthand the effort required to become a reader and witnessed the joy of unlocking the magic of words. Literacy was the delight of readers who immersed themselves in pages of books and began the journey as lifelong readers. This book is a culmination of my years of experience and expertise, designed to empower parents and caregivers to foster a love for reading in their children.

It Begins with a Book is your "hands-on" guide, whether you're a homeschooler or part of the traditional schooling system. It's your quick go-to for information, suggestions, and encouragement to raise your little readers. Having recently emerged from a worldwide pandemic where lives were upended, children attended school at home on computers, and parents struggled to balance work, school, and home environment, we learned quickly how life can become chaotic. We have settled back into everyday routines but discovered that the post-Covid era brings new challenges. Many children lost two years of social growth and solid academic instruction.

In addition, we have seen the rise of homeschool education. As families begin the homeschool journey, they may need suggestions for ways to promote literacy. With its practical tips and engaging activities, this book encourages a fresh approach to literacy at home, fostering a love for reading in both homeschooled and traditional schooling. From birth to elementary-age children, you'll find something for everyone!

And it gets better; you'll also discover the thread of creative literacy woven throughout this book. Creative literacy is not just about reading, it's about experiencing a book. When we can make a moment a memory, we plant something inside our children that keeps their interests blooming. This book contains the tools that parents need to nurture growth. I have gathered the seeds, the soil, and the array of colors that will grace the garden. Now, you can implement these tidbits at home, little by little, to grow your young readers. And the best part is—*It Begins with a Book*!

Get Started Early

Get Started Early

We can begin reading with our littles at birth! This section highlights some research and recommendations to prepare our homes for our littlest readers. We will explore what, when, and how to introduce books to little ones, along with suggestions for building a home library. There's no time to wait; let's get started early!

This Much is True

The library has 455 books. On Monday, 123 were taken out, and on Tuesday, 87 were returned. Children gathered for a read-aloud on Wednesday, and 62 books were checked out on Thursday. On Friday, 30 books were returned, and the library was full on Saturday. No one checked out books on Sunday because the library was closed. How many children have books?

Does this word problem get your mathematical wheels turning? Does it harken back to elementary school? Did you immediately start calculating the number of books or read the whole problem first before trying to solve it? Was there enough information to solve, and did you catch the hidden meaning in the wording?

When we look at this math problem we see numbers, but it also incorporates words such as library, read-aloud, and children. Some people gravitate toward words and books. Others toward numbers and research. We need both! Some of you want the data on why we need to raise little readers so I'm about to tell you. The key takeaway is the priority of books and the profound impact we can make when reading to our kids. Let's start with brain development!

As we examine research on the benefits of reading to our children, we need to understand the role of brain development in reading. Brain development is paramount in helping our children acquire the pre-reading and language skills necessary for becoming readers.

In a brain-based learning segment of *Edutopia*, an article by Rishi Sriram, "Why Ages 2-7 Matter So Much for Brain Development," explains that children's brains develop in spurts called critical periods. These are times in a child's life when they are receptive to certain types of learning, such as language acquisition and cognitive development. The first critical period occurs around age two and concludes around age seven. There are twice as many synapses in two-year-olds as in adults, indicating that during this phase, children can experience lasting effects on their development. The article states, "Children's brains can uniquely absorb information during this critical phase."[1] This could mean that introducing literature to children in their early years may allow them to absorb it more effectively, making it more likely they will engage with it later in life.

The American Academy of Pediatrics, a renowned institution in child health, has spent years advocating the importance of parents reading with children. In December 2024, they published a policy statement and technical report, saying:

Reading together often with infants and young children strengthens their relationships with parents and caregivers at a critical time in child development, stimulating brain circuitry and early attachment. A positive parenting practice, shared reading helps build the foundation for healthy social-emotional, cognitive, language, and literacy development, setting the stage for school readiness and providing enduring benefits across the life course. [2]

Additionally, in an article from the *Child Mind Institute*, Hannah Sheldon-Dean, shares powerful words from a clinical expert. "'Just exposure to words is the single most important thing that you can do to help build the language pathways in your child's brain,' says Laura Phillips, neuropsychologist PsyD. 'Reading and exposure to words help kids maximize their language and cognitive capacity.'" [3]

While numerous articles contain research and statistics, here are the key points and benefits of reading to children from birth.

- Opportunities for parent-child bonding

- Supports literacy engagement through shared reading experiences

- Provides preschoolers with some of the words they need to hear (21,000 a day)

- Exposes children to hundreds of thousands of words by the time they reach kindergarten
- Potential advantage in the acquisition of pre-reading skills
- Establishes daily routines
- Improves language and comprehension
- Fosters multi-lingual learning
- Six minutes a day can reduce stress
- Teaches littles and parents new things
- Aides in social and emotional growth
- Encourages a love of books and reading

Research and data can guide our decisions and actions. But no matter how we analyze the numbers, evaluate the data, and pore over the research, the key takeaway is that reading to our little ones from birth has enduring benefits!

Grow: Research provides evidence of the benefits of reading to our children; the bottom line is to start reading when they're babies and keep reading!

It Begins at Birth

Instilling a love of reading begins before birth! You are your child's first teacher. You have the first opportunity to create a love of literacy for your little ones. While mama is pregnant, she can read aloud to her unborn child. This steady rhythmic cadence will soothe the little one as they hear mama's voice.

Plus, a small purchase of one board book a week will begin to build that baby's library. Board books are now available in all sorts of places. You can find them at any large bookstore chain, local everyday store, favorite online distributor, discount stores, and even thrift stores. Board books are great for ages 0-3! At this age, children are exploring books. They are very tactile, and board books are sturdy enough to endure drool, sticky fingers, and the treasures of tiny hands.

When you choose your books, remember that having variety creates a dynamic personal library. Just as adults choose to read various texts, children are the same. Adults often choose to read novels, memoirs, magazines, internet articles, scientific journals, inspirational stories, self-help guides, and work-related texts.

Children enjoy variety as well! You can stock your home library with classics, favorite characters, a series, new finds, fiction, nonfiction, educational books, books in your native language, and faith-based stories.

It's important to remember that books should be of high interest to your children. When we create a love of literacy, we allow our children to participate in selecting their books. There is power in choice! Not all books in a library need to be silly, goofy, or fun, but you can assist your littles in selecting stories that will enhance their lives. When we foster a love of reading, we create lifelong learners.

The journey isn't always easy. Reading with babies and toddlers can be trying. The short attention span paired with lots of activity makes it hard to get through any significant amount of text.

It's good to begin by letting your baby explore books. Holding, turning, touching, and even crawling on are all excellent ways for your baby to experience literature. If you'd like to make it more interesting, you can turn the pages, make up the text, or point and talk about the pictures.

What is important is that you both are together with the books. As your child ages one or two years, they should be able to turn pages with you and sit for a short story (let's say two minutes). It's perfectly fine to break up the book into multiple readings. And often, your toddler will repeatedly choose the same book. So, you may have to be creative when introducing new stories.

While we nurture our children's love of reading, we can also support their development by establishing reading routines. Many families read before nap and bedtime, an ideal time to set aside to read with your child. They are a captive audience, beginning to settle down into rest. But you can also select other times throughout your day to incorporate reading: before or after dinner, a mid-morning break, or a mid-afternoon break. As a family, you can choose a routine that best suits you!

For school-age children, ages 5 – 8, there are designated times for literature experiences, often after recess or lunch, during a literacy block, weekly library visits, and independent reading time. These routines create predictability, set boundaries, promote stamina, and encourage time on task. Children this age also benefit from at-home reading routines.

It's essential to provide daily opportunities to interact with books. A book basket near the toys and a few tucked into the car or a backpack will allow children to interact with stories spontaneously too! In just fifteen to twenty minutes a day, you can help establish a foundation for lifelong reading.

Grow: We begin to instill a love of reading at birth when we select various books, encourage our little ones, and establish routines for daily reading.

When Parents Model Reading

Whether you realize it or not, books impacted you when you were little. You formulated ideas and opinions about reading in a negative, positive, or perhaps even indifferent manner while young. And you may still hold those feelings to this day!

Think about it . . . are you an avid reader? Are you anxious for the next new release on Tuesday mornings? Do you have a favorite author or genre? Do you casually scroll through social media posts, entertainment news, and current events? Or do you read exclusively for content, work-related text as required for your profession? Or any combination of the above? Regardless of how and what you read, each day you are reading, and every day your children are watching.

Little ones have big eyes. They watch every move you make; whether you realize it or not, they often imitate what you do. If you eat a cookie, they want a cookie. If you turn on the TV, they will want to watch TV. If you scroll on your phone, they will probably want to see your device. And while much of what we do is simply part of everyday life, we can certainly be intentional about how we model our behavior in front of our children. For example, eating a healthy snack or walking instead of watching TV in the morning. The same is true for reading!

Reading to your child is fantastic, and we have established the value of this practice. But it's incredibly powerful for your child to see you read independently. If your little one is old enough to sit with books for a few minutes, you can begin to establish a daily routine of reading your book right next to them. As they age (around 18 months to 2 years old), they become more independent with books and can look at pictures. You can increase the time you read together in small increments, and before you know it, you might have ten minutes of reading your book next to your child as they "read."

You show them the value of sitting down with a book by modeling reading. Your actions demonstrate that reading is important and enjoyable. As mentioned earlier, research shows that six minutes of daily reading reduces stress. We can all agree that is a benefit!

Grow: Model good reading behavior for your child by sitting adjacent to them with your book as they read their book.

The House on Olive Avenue

It stood felicitously on the corner of Olive Avenue, a Victorian-style home built in the early 1900s. It was a brilliant sight, with small steps leading to a quaint porch that may have housed rocking chairs and a glass of lemonade on a scorching August afternoon. The entryway was simple, but the staircase was inviting. Several steps led up to a most spectacular room that was a haven for books, and this personal library held hundreds! The best part was that I could borrow whichever one I wanted.

Bernice Roberts, a retired kindergarten teacher, owned the house on Olive Avenue. Her gentle demeanor and warm welcome made it feel like visiting grandma's house. She graciously invited my brother and me for a few visits, and those visits are forever etched in my literary heart. Bernice was the first to introduce Beatrix Potter and the characters of Peter Rabbit, Mr. McGregor, Squirrel Nutkin, and Jeremy Fisher. I was enamored, engaged, and enchanted!

This house on Olive Avenue, whose owner was gracious enough to share her treasures, had provided a new book experience. She opened the door to a world of wonder and literacy, and as a young girl, I was thrilled. I had always been an avid reader, and in this era of my life, I immersed myself in books and the kindness of a booklover, which was where a shift began.

Books became more than just stories; they were opportunities to explore, imagine, and indulge myself in times and spaces beyond my elementary-age world. I read everything I could, plunging head-first into the depths of novels. The transformative power of books was evident. I spent countless hours reading books from the library, my classroom, and the ones my parents bought me.

My love of books began and blossomed in childhood, and my rich literacy experiences helped spark an enduring love for reading. I have started a reading room of my own to begin reading room moments while bonding over books. And I have several friends who have done the same!

While my memories of the reading room might be embellished, and I may have omitted a few details in my description of her home, I can credit some of my love of stories to the woman in the house on Olive Avenue. I'm inspired to create similar moments and memories for young readers and their families. So now that you've read my story about a reading room let's get you on your way to building your home library!

Grow: Create reading room moments with family members and build bonding memories over books!

Building a Home Library

I was an eager young mama who desired to set my littles up for success. I spent hours poring over my *What to Expect When You're Expecting* book to prepare for each of my babies' arrivals. I followed recommendations for my health, nursery preparation, and the best ways to support my babies in the first years of life. I began planning, buying, and receiving items here and there, adding them to our collection of all things—baby! Does this sound familiar?

Dreams, ideas, blueprints, design, décor, room size—you've gone to great lengths to ensure your baby's first room is perfect. You've set everything in motion: the crib, changing table, dresser, rocking chair, brand-new baby clothes (that won't fit for another eight months), toy basket full of stuffies, and the first-year developmentally appropriate toys. You feel confident and accomplished! All that's left now is to bring this little one into the world. But wait, you forgot something—books!

Books are an essential accoutrement to your baby's living space and bringing them in is easier than you may think. Perhaps you've been given a few books as shower gifts and may have purchased a few throughout your pregnancy. Perfect! You're on your way to building a home library. One of the best ways to create a little reader is to start young. It's simple but important because we start at birth. And when we want to encourage reading, it begins with a book!

A Case for Board Books

My daughters are in their thirties now, so we had limited access to board books when they were young, mainly because there weren't many. Today, there is a wide variety of available board books. I can assure you that I collected over one hundred when my grandson was a toddler, and they served us well.

Board books are a must for newborns, infants, and even toddlers. These books are small, durable, and travel well. They are often a condensed version of a longer story, which is excellent for toddlers' and preschoolers' shorter attention spans. You can tuck a few into toy bins and play tubs as a fun way to integrate creative play and books.

Let's focus on the variety of books we can add to our home library. Here are some suggestions that can guide you as you begin.

- **ABC's** – a great way to begin setting a foundation for literacy

- **123's** – and while you're at it, start those math skills, too

- **Colors** – keep little eyes immersed in the hues of our world

- **Animals** – who doesn't love them? Animal babies are always a hit

- **Babies in action** – babies love to see other babies

- **Interactive tactile books** and **lift-the-flap books** – like *That's Not My Reindeer*

- **Patterned text or books from songs** like: "No More Monkeys Jumping on the Bed" or "The Wheels on the Bus"

- **Predictable** – books that allow children to anticipate what is next, like *Brown Bear, Brown Bear, What Do You See?*

- **Classics** – tried and true favorites like *Goodnight Moon* and *The Runaway Bunny*

- **Picture books** that have become board books: *Llama, Llama Red Pajama* or *Sheep in a Jeep*

- **New Favorites** – *Little Blue Truck* series

- **Holiday books** – there are oodles of board books available for each holiday

- **Faith-based books** – first Bible stories, characters from the Bible, books about God, prayer books, and stories that teach character traits of faith

- **Educational** – Baby Signing (a book about sign language), STEM, stories in other languages

Remember, these suggestions are meant to encourage diversity for you and your little ones. Each time you add a book to your home library, you increase the opportunity for your little one to love literacy. So, add one or several, but keep building one book at a time!

Grow: Choose a variety of board books as you build a home library for your littles!

Read, Read, Read

Read, Read, Read

The best thing we can do to grow little readers is read! As we embark on the joyful reading journey for our kids, we benefit from tips and tools to help us. We want to read daily, and we want our children to engage in the stories we read. This section will dive into book experiences and ways to involve our littles in literature. And the best way to do that is to read, read, read!

Book Rotations and Bedside Baskets

It's a small condominium—1,000 square feet at best—but somehow, this family of four has managed to fill it with bundles of items and boatloads of toys. Mama gingerly steps over figurines, gadgets from the play kitchen, dollhouse accessories, stuffies, and more. Frustration rises as she reaches the bedroom. Although adept at navigating this toy trail, she decides that something needs to change. Can you relate?

While the toys invite hours of play, they also create a glorious mess. Inevitably, this mama develops a system to organize everything, creating order out of chaos. She starts "toy rotations." Once a month, she puts some toys away and brings out different ones. Of course, favorites are always on hand because kids like what they like. And to her surprise, toys became more enjoyable and easier to manage.

Why do I tell you this? The same concept of toy rotations works wonderfully with books. Book rotations!

My grandson has oodles of books. His mama has a wooden book organizer in his room that simultaneously displays ten to twelve books. In addition, there are books on shelves and in baskets. Books, books, books! Every few weeks, she switches out stories to keep reading routines engaging. This effective system of organizing keeps books fresh and also holds interest.

Have you tried this? I highly recommend it. Throughout the year, note holidays, events, and themes to help with book selections for the month. You will likely discover that book rotations give you more opportunities to read the numerous stories you have collected over the year.

Another way to organize books and encourage reading before rest is with a bedside basket. Choose a basket that will hold several books, and then let your child select the titles to put inside. Consider switching out the books weekly to maximize the use of your library. Another option would be to place stories you've checked out from your local library inside the basket. A reading tub or bin would work well too. You can organize your basket by theme, holidays, nonfiction, board books, picture books, and chapter books when your children are older.

Reading to children before nap and bedtime is part of traditional routines, which is fantastic! It's a great time to help little ones settle down before sleep and an opportunity for them to hear parents reading aloud. Listening to reading is a valuable and important skill for children as they become readers. It allows kids to hear fluent reading and builds listening comprehension. But it also nurtures a bond and connection between parents and little ones.

What if your little one is transitioning out of naps but still needs downtime? A bedside basket can help! Perhaps you can set "rest time" for your child. Choosing books to read during quiet time can provide children with a peaceful and calming experience. You can set a timer and encourage your child to read or look at the pictures of the books in their bedside basket until they hear the timer ring.

Get creative but remember to have your little ones to participate—this is the best way to get "buy-in" for reading!

Grow: Keep books fresh and organized with book rotations while you encourage reading with a bedside basket before rest.

Read It Once, Read It Twice!

Have you been to Starbucks, McDonald's, or Chick-fil-A? Have you been more than once? More than ten times? Do you get something new each time or always order the same thing? Why do you go back to a place where you've already been?

Some reasons might include taste and flavor, convenience, affordability, preference, proximity, and family favorite.

I live near Disneyland, yes, the Magic Kingdom! When I was little, my family visited several times. I loved it! When I had my children, I decided Disneyland would be a staple in our recreational fun.

My daughters loved Disney as much as I did, and we had annual passes for several years. Why did we go back to Disneyland so often? I can assure you it wasn't for convenience or affordability. But it was near our home (proximity); we enjoyed it more than the other amusement parks nearby (preference), and it was a family favorite. Not to mention the sounds, sights, and smells that ignite nostalgia and whimsy when you walk through the gates. And each time we went, we discovered something new!

You are probably wondering what on earth this has to do with reading. Books are like a favorite restaurant or destination. They bring comfort, predictability, and often new discoveries. When we read stories that are familiar, our littles can participate in reading along with us. They will learn the pattern of the text and repeat their favorite parts. They may even uncover hidden treasures in artwork that the illustrator has gone to great lengths to create. Favorite books are convenient and affordable because they likely live right under our roofs and are often just a quick grab away. So read them once, read them twice!

Do your littles have a favorite book? Have you read it once or maybe twice? Maybe you've read it so many times you don't even need to look at the words! Why not let your child read to you? Let them read aloud the words they have memorized. Have them retell or recall essential events in the story. Or perhaps help your little one look for something new in the story you hadn't seen in previous readings. There is value in revisiting a familiar story; just like our favorite coffee shop, we'll go back again and again. So, that book that your little one insists on each night? Well, read it once, read it twice!

Grow: Reading and rereading a familiar book provides opportunities for your children to memorize text patterns, repeat and recall story details, and discover something new!

Book Buddies and Take-Along Totes

Perched on the edge of her bed, she pulls out a carefully detailed list. Eyes glancing back and forth from the bed to the list, she whispers, "It's your turn!"

As he watches from the doorway, her dad's curiosity can't be contained. "Hey, little one, what are you doing? You're supposed to be choosing your books for bedtime stories."

"I know, Dad. But first, I need to see which stuffed animal sleeps beside my pillow tonight."

Dad nods knowingly and scoots several furry friends to the back of her bed as he opens a book for a bedtime story. Snuggling in close with the honored stuffie in her lap, she leans in and listens as her dad begins to read.

Do you know a little one who loves stuffed animals as much as the child in the above story? Littles love stuffies, and they are great companions during story time. Animal and character stuffies are available in all shapes and sizes, and you can find them in many retail locations or online.

Stuffed animals make great book buddies. Having a stuffed animal to cuddle up with as you read is fun. They are snuggly, soft, good listeners, and they never interrupt! If your child has begun to read, practicing reading fluency with their stuffed animals can ease some nerves.

Looking for ideas for a birthday or holiday gift? Stuffed animals combined with a new book make wonderful presents. Bookstores often display these combos, which makes your shopping easier. Just be sure to select the age-appropriate pair!

Book buddies are fantastic in a basket with books, but they also love to travel. You can put them in the car for a ride or in a suitcase for a getaway. Bring book buddies with you and let them enjoy books too. Looking for a clever way to carry them? Try a take-along tote!

Take-along totes are "carriers" for your books and stuffies. They provide a convenient way to transport these combinations for your little ones. You can use plastic totes, different-sized backpacks, purses, diaper bags, and fabric totes. Almost anything large enough to hold a book and a stuffie (and has a handle) will work for a take-along tote!

Grow: Stuffed animals are terrific book buddies, gifts, and for on-the-go!

The Value of Wonder

Do you know what kids are really good at? Asking questions! They are innately curious about the world around them, and often, once they've asked one question, they have another that follows. If you've ever spent time with a three-year-old, you know exactly what I'm talking about. It goes something like this:

Adult: Look at that butterfly! See how it flies?
Three-year-old: Why does it fly?
Adult: Well, that's what a butterfly does.
Three-year-old: Why?
Adult: Because it has to get food.
Three-year-old: Why?
Adult: It needs food to stay alive; it sips nectar from the flowers.
Three-year-old: Which flower?
Adult: I'm not sure. I guess any flower.
Three-year-old: Then what does it do?
Adult: It rests, I suppose.
Three-year-old: Why?
Adult: Because it's tired.
Three-year-old: Where does it rest?

Adult: Maybe on a leaf or a branch.

Three-year-old: Why?

Adult: So, it can give its wings a chance to rest when it sits. It's not flying, so it gets a break.

Three-year-old: Why does it need a break?

Adult: Because it's tired, just like I am right now! I have an idea; let's get some books about butterflies. That will help us both!

Simple answers and explanations placate some children while others persist in their barrage of questions. If you have the latter, you have a treasure. Curiosity is a gift and one that doesn't always last as long as we may wish. Use these questions from your littles to guide you as you select your next books. What are their interests? What do they enjoy? What keeps them questioning? Don't stop once they turn four. Keep tapping into the interests of your littles, keep learning, and keep asking questions!

Grow: Asking and answering questions is a great way to foster curiosity in your child and will help you choose books that interest your little one!

ELEMENOP–Letters and literacy

A-B-C-D-E-F-G, H-I-J-K . . .

L - M - N -O -P! Introducing the alphabet is an essential part of education at home. It's safe to say we have all sung this song at some point in our lives and, for many of us, ad nauseum.

While it's a catchy little tune and a clever way to teach our littles the letters of the alphabet, it's not the only way. Did you know there are many creative ways to prepare your littles with letter recognition and, eventually, the foundation of reading? Of course, books will be an essential resource and assist you as you're introducing letters.

But hands-on letter manipulatives will create an extension of your alphabet experience. Toddlers and preschoolers are often ready to extend a reading activity with letter tools. Below are a few suggestions for letter tools your child can use while you are reading.

- Alphabet puzzles – chunky letters
- Magnet letters
- Foamy letters

- Cookie cutter letters

- Playdoh letters

- Alphabet stamps

*(As a parent, grandparent, educator, or caregiver, **you must ensure your little one is safe**. Be sure to gauge this appropriately. Age recommendations are often listed on the packaging of items.)*

Reading an alphabet story can become an interactive activity. For example, you can read *Chicka, Chicka Boom Boom* aloud and have your child find the matching letters as you read. Or you can read *LMNO Peas* and have your kiddo create Play-Doh letters for each page. Using manipulatives taps into another part of your child's learning. The kinesthetic and tactile interaction paired with the auditory and visual experience takes your read-aloud to a new level.

Here are a few books that you could use for this activity:

Chicka Chicka Boom Boom
Alphaprints ABC
ABC's of Kindness
Eating the Alphabet
The Very Hungry Caterpillar ABC
Dr. Seuss ABC
Cement Mixer's ABC: (Goodnight, Goodnight Construction Site)

Alphabet Mystery
LMNO Peas
Alpha Oops! The Day Z Went First
A to Z by Sandra Boynton

As your children get older, they will become familiar with letters and begin to read and write them. You can use a whiteboard, paper and crayons, sand, clay, and skywriting (drawing in the air with your finger). PreK and kindergarteners can turn the book's pages and create the letters. They might even be able to read some of the words with you. And now, when you think of the Alphabet Song, it might even bring a little smile to your face!

Grow: Use age-appropriate manipulatives with your littles as you're teaching them the alphabet!

Old MacDonald Had a Farm—Books and Creative Play

It was a typical weekday morning with my grandson. His mama dropped him off to go to work while he and I played before preschool. We had the plastic farm, animals, and tractors set out, and we were ready for some good 'ol farm fun. Moving the farmer and animals in the play area, we sang "Old MacDonald Had a Farm" as we acted out movements and practiced our best animal noises. As we sang, my eyes caught the book basket, and I noticed a book about the farm. I grabbed it, flipped it open, and began to read. It was a counting book, so we used our animals to count along as we read. We finished that book, and I found one more farm book with photos of actual animals. He matched his plastic cow to the picture of the cow in the book, the horse, the pig, etc. So fun!

This moment was an epiphany for me. Have you ever considered bringing books into playtime with your little ones? I hadn't either until that day! We turned our fifteen-minute activity into an hour-long event. He was almost four, so his "on-task" attention span was longer than a toddler's. But this would work the same with younger children if you shortened the timeframe to fifteen to thirty minutes. Need some ideas to get you started?

Here are some examples:

*Howdy, Partner!

My grandson and I loved to play with Potato Head. We would try to outdo each other by creating silly faces with our potatoes. And sometimes, we made personalities such as comedians, pirates, athletes, or farmers. One day, while having fun with the many faces of Potato, we went through our books and found book characters to match our potato creations! It was a fantastic way to extend our creative playtime and add literacy.

*One, two, three, four - I spy a dinosaur

We have a cool sand tub with plastic dinosaurs. You can bury them and then search for them in the sand. It's a messy activity, so it stays outside, not where you traditionally read books. But why not read books outdoors too? Let's think beyond the usual reading spots! There are oodles of books about dinosaurs, many of them with multisyllabic names that are difficult to pronounce (so get your mouth ready). But I have found that children are often better at memorizing the names and types of dinosaurs than adults. Books about dinosaurs are available in fiction and no-fiction. You can find them for children of all ages!

*Dress up, tea parties and more

Little ones love to pretend, and many love to dress up! A great way to incorporate a book into play is to read stories such as *Fancy Nancy* or *Pinkalicious* and let your child dress up like the character. Perhaps you'd like to organize a tea party for a few of your child's friends and allow them to dress up as part of the fun! Set up a small table or create a space on a protected surface (floor with a tablecloth), get some cute paper plates and cups, and let the littles have a tea party with lemonade and cookies.

There are many creative ways to bring books into playtime. Let's step outside the box and think differently about reading and play with our littles.

Grow: Bring books into playtime to extend and enhance learning and creativity as your child plays.

I Spy with My Little Eye—Wordplay

Sitting at the breakfast table one morning, her son mumbles, "Mama, look at that fat cat!"

Mama notices the cat and giggles with a reply, "Yes, look at that! It's a fat cat!"

She continues with the wordplay by pointing out her three rhyming words. "Listen to these words—that, fat, cat. They all sound the same! Can you hear it?"

Her son listens intently and begins to mimic. "That, fat, cat."

"Yes!" Mama replies. "Let's see if we can find other words that rhyme. What about fat, cat, hat—"

But, before she can finish, her son jumps in, "Hop!"

Mama pauses and then slowly repeats the four words, "Fat, cat, hat, hop. Hmm, that doesn't sound right. Let's try it in a sentence: The fat cat wore a . . . hat or hop?"

With a grin, her little guy chimes, "The fat cat wore a hat!"

"That's right!" Mama cheers. "We found three words that rhyme: fat, cat, and hat. Can we come up with more? What about bat?

Her son repeats the four rhyming words and then adds his own at the end of the word string: "fat, cat, hat, bat, and mat."

"Terrific! You did it! You made five words that rhyme."

Mama and her son created a moment of phonological awareness that began organically at the breakfast table. These skills are the building blocks for the foundation of reading, and they can start at home. Mama doesn't need to be a teacher to capture an opportunity to play a word game with her son. Conversations at the table, in the car, or during playtime can provide plenty of opportunities for wordplay. Imagine mama and son having more time to continue their breakfast game. It could look like this:

"Now, let's change this game and see if we can find words that start with 'h,' like hat and hop, and—hmmmm, how about hippo!" smiles Mama.

Eager to jump into this new wordplay game, he shouts, "I know a word: house. And horse."

Mama thinks for a moment and says, "Hamburger."

The game continues back and forth until they switch to a new letter, focusing on each word's beginning letter. Hearing the beginning sounds of a word and then reproducing the sound by choosing a word that follows the beginning letter is another way to extend learning.

Generally speaking, children ages three to four can comprehend and participate in rhyming games. Nursery rhymes, songs, and books for little ones contain rhyming words, which builds a bridge to practicing rhyming aloud with littles. Isolating sounds at the beginning of a word is a more challenging skill that develops as children age.

Please note: Children develop language skills at different levels and timeframes. Not all children rhyme or isolate beginning sounds at the exact same age. Some acquire these skills early, and others a bit later. The emphasis should be on engaging your little one in wordplay from an early age, understanding that each child's journey is unique!

Grow: Wordplay with rhyming and beginning letter sounds creates moments of phonological awareness, which begins to build a foundation for reading!

Lions and Tigers and Bears, Oh My!— Nonfiction Delights

Did you know that giraffes are the tallest animals on land? Their legs are as tall as a grown man's. Their necks are just as tall. If you add in their bodies, that means that giraffes can be 14 to 19 feet tall.[1]

Nonfiction deserves a seat of honor on every bookshelf in a library! Why? Because this is the place where littles learn about the world around them. It offers real photos, facts, and even trivia about our world and the creatures, plants, and life that surround it. There are tons of nonfiction stories and books to share with your children. Even at the youngest age, you can introduce nonfiction to your kids to expand their learning journey.

For the littlest, you can begin with board books that show babies in real life. Babies love babies! They may mimic or display interest in what the babies are doing. Animal-baby books are also fun for this age group, making the learning process enjoyable for both you and your child.

Toddlers enjoy books about the world around them, such as transportation, families, animals, community, and daily life. At this age, we can encourage children to point to specific photos in the book and begin to ask questions about the book.

Preschool and elementary age nonfiction books offer text that provides information about the pictures they see. Captions, maps, diagrams, vocabulary, and indexes will assist this group of readers as they navigate the wonders of nonfiction. Reading nonfiction may lead to opportunities for further exploration and learning.

Nonfiction is outstanding for a read-aloud, as well! Parents can support comprehension by asking questions during and after reading. In addition, pausing to highlight new vocabulary or to discuss facts will further engage kids in the reading experience. And for extra credit, look for a fictional story that complements your nonfiction text!

Giraffes Can't Dance (fiction) *Nat Geo Kids - Giraffes* (nonfiction)
Dinosaurs (nonfiction) *How Do Dinosaurs Say Goodnight?* (fiction)

When children are old enough to compare and contrast fiction and nonfiction, you've created a moment of extension in learning. Questions such as: How were these books similar? How were the books different? What tells you that this book is "make-believe"? Is there anything factual in this fiction story?

Do animals talk in real life? What did you learn? Is there anything more you'd like to know?

Grow: Nonfiction books offer insight into real life and introduce little ones to the world around them.

Building a Home Library—Part Two

Picture books are fabulous when building a home library! Generally, they contain thirty-two pages of creative storytelling and colorful artwork. Picture books combine the beautiful blend of an author's inspired words with the brilliant images an artist dreams up. The combination is a literary delight!

So, when is the right time to introduce picture books to our children, and how do we transition from board books to picture books?

Picture books are best suited for children ages 3 – 8 and are available in hardback, paperback, and e-book formats. The hardback format, with its sturdy cover, is often long-lasting, but it is the most expensive purchase of the three. Paperbacks are easy to carry and stack, and they are more affordable. E-books are great for devices and taking stories on the go. Perhaps your child's library could include an assortment of all three.

Introducing picture books to a young child should be intentional. It is a perfect opportunity to instruct and inform your little one on the fragility of pages in a picture book and the proper way to hold a book. Let them feel the pages and show them the difference between a durable board book and the thin pages of a picture book. Allow your little one to demonstrate gentle hands and care with picture books and have them practice holding the book. You can model this for your child and then let them try. Careful page-turning and storage will keep books safe and ready to be enjoyed for years.

At first, little ones will be prone to quick page-turning due to a short attention span. A few minutes at a time will be a reading goal when you begin picture book reading. You can even read a picture book in sections, dividing it into separate readings. As your child ages and becomes more mature, they can attend to the text for an extended time. Take cues from your little one and pause when they become disengaged. Remember, we don't want them to be disinterested; we are trying to create lifelong readers! And, of course, celebrate the array of stories now available by adding picture books to your daily reading routine!

Grow: Picture books provide creative storytelling and colorful artwork to engage little readers with thirty-two pages of literary delight!

Optimize Opportunities

<u>Optimize Opportunities</u>

Once we have established routines, encouraged our little ones to read, and created reading experiences, we will start to see a transition toward reading independence. While we celebrate this milestone, we need to stay connected to the stories and books our children read. Jump in to see how we can optimize our opportunities to keep kids reading!

Enchanted Readers

harlotte's Web was the first chapter book she ever read. As a six-year-old reading the book cover to cover, she was certain she should live on a farm like Fern and raise a baby pig named Wilbur. She was enchanted! From then on, she immersed herself in all sorts of chapter books, spending hours imagining that she was the main character in every book and living in the middle of the setting with each plot unfolding before her. She read everything!

Children who are enchanted readers will find that reading is an adventure. Enchanted readers seek out new stories and are content to read on their own without prompting or prodding from parents or teachers. They love to read for pleasure and are often annoyed if they must stop for routine activities such as chores, meals, events, recess, or lunch.

In my experience, enchanted readers are pleased to talk about what they are reading with others, be it parents, teachers, or peers. They are great role models in a classroom setting because they are often seen with a book. Enchanted readers may have stronger vocabulary skills, comprehension, and even writing abilities because they have so much experience with text. As the adage says, "The more you read, the better you write."

Do you have an enchanted reader? If you have a child who is an enchanted reader, then you know the joy of watching them interact with stories daily. You may have invested time and money to keep your reader engaged and know that having an enchanted reader can be a delight!

But did you know you can continue to foster that love of reading by engaging your child in conversations about their books? Ask questions, have them summarize a chapter, share a favorite section, and give an opinion about the book. As a parent, caregiver, or grandparent, you can spur on the love of literature when you show interest in what they read!

Grow: If you have an enchanted reader, spur on their love of reading with questions about their books and interest in their stories.

Resolute Readers

Having an enchanted reader is a joy, but what about children who haven't found the magic of a book? Some children struggle with reading because they find it hard to understand the stories and the "work" of reading gets in the way of their enjoyment.

These children might be called struggling readers, but I prefer to see them as resolute readers. While teaching, I worked closely with all types of readers, including those who had yet to unlock the code of reading. I observed these readers and the tremendous effort it took to read. It was important to understand their challenges and provide the proper support. Here are some of my observations:

- Below grade-level readers must be diligent in their approach to reading.

- They often put in more effort to decode and decipher the letter sound combinations.

- Students who don't read fluently may have difficulty understanding the text they read.

- Some students who aren't reading grade-level text have lower self-esteem because they compare themselves to their on grade-level peers.

- Students "learn to read" until grade 3, then reading shifts, and "they read to learn." Grade 3 is a pivotal year.

I taught in a public school, using assessments, remediation, small group instruction, reading intervention strategies, and one-on-one support when needed. My job was to teach and assist students in their reading. I had extensive training, and teaching reading was my passion!

Most parents will not be instructing their children in the fundamentals of reading. However, parents can play a pivotal role by creating a love of literature early in life. The first five years of a child's life are pivotal, so introducing books and reading to them daily while young is a perfect starting point. As children begin school, parents can continue reading daily and support the skills they acquire as little readers. Regardless of reading ability, parents can inspire their children with words of affirmation, empathy with challenges, and partnership in shared reading experiences. While I can't prescribe or promise a perfect outcome, I can say with confidence that children benefit when they are supported and encouraged to read in a school or home environment.

Grow: Offer ample opportunities and oodles of encouragement for your little reader who grows each day!

Reluctant Readers—Offer Them Choices

"No, you're not having chocolate chip pancakes for dinner."

"Yes, you must wear a helmet when you ride your bike."

"No, you can't stay up until 10 p.m. You're only six years old."

"Because I said so!"

"I'm the parent, and I know what's best."

"No, that book is ridiculous. You're not reading it!"

Do any of these phrases sound familiar? Have you uttered any of them either out loud or under your breath? Me too! As a parent and educator, I've been in your shoes. I understand the challenges and the importance of setting boundaries for the well-being of our children. Sometimes, we face a barrage of unreasonable requests and must be firm with our responses. Many decisions parents make are non-negotiable, as they should be. Parents have a tough job and must be the ultimate authority. We have the privilege and responsibility of raising our children well.

While it's essential to maintain your stance on your child's safety, health, and overall well-being, you might find opportunities to collaborate with your child in some decision-making (within reason, of course). For example, when your child requests chocolate chip pancakes for dinner, you might offer them for dessert. If your little one wants to stay up late, perhaps you'd be willing to extend a child's bedtime on a Friday evening when it's not a school night. And if your child wants to read a book that you don't like, take a moment to listen to the "why" behind their choice, explain your thoughts on your decision, and discuss alternative literature.

Children love to choose! They like to choose their toys, clothing, friends, activities, and even books they read. But some children don't want to choose books because they don't like reading. These kiddos are <u>reluctant readers</u>! Unlike resolute readers, who have difficulty reading, reluctant readers are disengaged. They may be frustrated because they aren't entertained, the stories don't pique their interest, and they are required to read for school. Reluctant readers may claim to be "bored" with books because they haven't found the right one yet. The joy of reading is something we can help them discover, and allowing some choices in literature may reduce their reluctance.

Determining your child's interests can be an influential strategy for reluctant readers, and parent involvement in book choices is crucial! Parents need to know what their kids are reading. I recommend previewing the text before allowing children to read. You can use sites such as Common Sense Media and Good Reads to research the suggested age range, Lexile levels (reading levels), and reviews of books. Reading material should be at or slightly above reading level to maintain comprehension unless a parent reads aloud with the child and facilitates discussion.

In the classroom, I found that my reluctant readers would gravitate toward books that mirrored what they watched on television; this was not my favorite, trust me! However, I wanted to create lifelong readers. I wanted to build on their interests, even if what they chose to read wasn't what I considered "quality" literature: books with rich vocabulary, strong character development, and solid plots.

Children won't always choose books with educational merit. While this is to the dismay of many educators and parents, exploring their interests and inquiring about the literature they enjoy is helpful. Understanding and respecting their interests, even if they differ from ours, is key to encouraging a love of reading.

Let me give you an example: imagine your little one loves superheroes. Did you know there are many books about superheroes at many different reading levels? We don't have to stack our shelves with superhero books and goofy stories, but we can certainly strike a balance in our home libraries, and allowing choices can motivate our little readers.

Grow: Allowing your child to choose some reading material can motivate them to stay engaged with books.

Independent and Not-So-Independent Readers

My Child Reads Independently

Congratulations, you've got a reader! It may have happened organically or with much determination and hard work. Still, you and your child should celebrate this significant milestone. You both are on your way to independence in literacy. Once your child begins to read independently, you may assume they will take full responsibility for books and daily reading, which is partially true. Newfound independence means that stories can be read and enjoyed without constant support. However, staying connected with your children's reading is still essential even with this new independence. Parents will want to inquire about the stories they are reading and listen as they read. One suggestion is to have your child read a chapter or part of the book aloud so you can listen to the reading fluency. Reading fluency is the rate at which they read. They should be reading aloud at a steady pace, just the way we speak. Reading fluency helps maintain comprehension, and in turn, this will help them become more confident in their reading.

My Child Doesn't Read Independently

Every child has their own timeline for unlocking the magic of reading. However, systematic practices are in place to facilitate the process. In a school setting, students will participate in phonemic awareness activities, phonics, and vocabulary building, including high-frequency words and sight words and blending letters that turn into sounds. Fluency and comprehension are also pieces of the reading puzzle. Direct instruction is most likely how your child will learn to read. It will happen smoothly and quickly for some children, while it takes more time for others. When there's a reluctance to begin the reading process, it's essential to continue to encourage your child. You can do this by reading together. You can boost good reading behavior when you carve out time for reading, allow your child to choose books, and take turns reading a story together.

Grow: Each child has their own timeline for unlocking the magic of reading, and once you have an independent reader, stay connected with your child's reading experiences!

Book Bandages: Stories That Help Heal

It's four a.m., and you wake to find your six-year-old standing at your bedside, grasping your hand with sweaty palms and wild eyes. You're sure this sweet child has had a nightmare and has come for reassurance. Sitting up in bed and pulling him close, you comfort him and offer gentle words. You'd like to walk him back to his bed, tuck him in, and return for an hour more of sleep when he insists that he hasn't had a bad dream but is worried about school. He has fears that keep him awake, and he is scared. Reality sinks in, and you understand his concern. The words you offer aren't enough, but you remember that he has a few books to address his struggle. Together, you walk to his room, turn on the light, grab a book from the shelf, and snuggle up to read a story about fears.

Books transport us to different times and places. Fiction lets us enter a world of make-believe, while nonfiction provides information about the world around us. Both genres have unique benefits. Sometimes, an author writes about a make-believe character experiencing a real-life conflict: realistic fiction. Realistic fiction can be a fantastic tool for families, primarily when the stories focus on social and emotional needs. The books below are a few examples of stories that address life's worries, fears, and uncertainties.

Chris and Lindsey Wheeler's story *Kit and the Missing Notebook*, tells the story of a kangaroo named Kit with anxiety. Her anxiety becomes heightened when her favorite notebook goes missing. Toward the end of the story, the authors describe how Kit manages her anxious thoughts: deep breathing in and out. As a bonus, they have included a note to families with strategies to cope with anxiety.

The Good Egg and *The Bad Seed* by Jory John feature inanimate objects as main characters. In *The Good Egg*, the main character struggles with perfectionism and pressure to care for others. When he begins to fall apart, he realizes that caring for his needs is essential. *The Bad Seed* has a reputation for, well, being bad. After a rough start in life, he becomes jaded and enjoys behaving poorly. But when he finally decides it's time to change his ways, he's pleasantly surprised at the response from others.

Another book series by authors Michelle Nietert and Tama Fortner addresses social and emotional needs. *God, I Feel Sad* and *God, I Feel Scared* offer support tools through language for children to identify, describe, and understand their feelings. In addition, both are terrific resources for families. And if faith is important to you, a reassurance of big feelings but a bigger God who sees and cares for you is a resounding theme of both books.

New beginnings bring excitement for some and worry for others. Books are a terrific tool for preparing, celebrating, and promoting positive school experiences while validating the emotions of little ones. Two fantastic stories, *Llama Llama Misses Mama* by Anna Dewdney and *The Kissing Hand* by Audrey Penn share the challenges of being away from mom and the reassurance of being reunited at the end of the school day.

Children who see themselves in a story feel valued, seen, and heard. If a character is experiencing something a child is going through, it creates a connection and a similarity, fostering empathy and understanding. No one wants to feel alone in their struggles. Books not only open doors to communication but also make these discussions more comfortable. They can be a beautiful bridge for open and honest conversations between children and parents about social and emotional issues.

Grow: Books about social and emotional issues can bridge conversations for parents and offer reassurance to children.

Willy Nilly, Silly Billy—Rhyming Stories

We looked!

Then we saw him step in on the mat!

We looked!

And we saw him!

The Cat in the Hat!

And he said to us,

"Why do you sit there like that?"

Dr. Seuss, *The Cat in the Hat*

I do not like them in a house. I do not like them with a mouse.

I do not like them here or there. I do not like them anywhere.

I do not like green eggs and ham. I do not like them Sam-I-am.

Dr. Seuss, *Green Eggs and Ham*

I joined a book club when I was pregnant with my oldest daughter. It was a Dr. Seuss book club, and I received new books in the mail each month. Delighted, I would read the titles aloud to my pregnant tummy, confident that my eloquence with rhyme would make a reader out of my little one. If the silly tongue twisters made me want to read them repeatedly, I was sure the same would be true for my child. I was spot on! My daughter had her favorites, and we read them over and over.

As a classroom teacher, I discovered that most students instantly connected with rhyming books. They would eagerly read along with me, and I would pause at the end of each line to allow them to speak the words. Rhyming text, with its predictability, not only keeps the reader engaged but also fosters a shared reading experience that is truly joyful and engaging.

Beyond the fun that emerges from books with rhyming words, we can use these books for the greater good. Did you know that books with rhyming words can build reading fluency? Reading fluency is reading a text correctly, with appropriate speed and expression. We teach kids to read the way we speak, not as robots and not as a race. Children can read books with rhyme to create a cadence and flow to their reading pattern. While you may be concerned that your child has "memorized" the text, even memorization will benefit readers who need to increase fluency.

Here's a fascinating challenge: take a moment to explore your child's library and count the number of rhyming books. You might be surprised how many children's authors write books in rhyme. Did you find a few? Several? Let your child pick one and embark on a reading adventure together!

Grow: Books written in rhyme can help build reading fluency!

What Happens Next?

Picture this: You're watching your favorite television se-ries, the one that's been on hiatus for six months. You're deeply involved in the characters and storyline when the plot thickens and "cut!" There's a break, and the show comes to an abrupt stop.

Wait! What happens next? Without realizing it, this week's episode ends and you must wait a week to discover what happens next. Why do writers and producers do this? One reason is that pausing at a pivotal point builds energy and excitement. It gets you thinking and talking about the potential outcomes. Those cliffhanger moments build momentum.

So, what would that look like when we read aloud to our kids? Imagine sitting with your child and reading a picture or chapter book. When you come to a problem, conflict, or climax of the book, pause your reading, and before you turn the page, ask your child, "What happens next?"

Let your child offer suggestions about what they imagine, observe, or wonder; this creates an opportunity for engagement with the text and conversations. Chances are your little one will have some interesting guesses. Some may be correct, and some may not—either way, it's a win because they are thinking about the story as you read. It gives you a window into your child's imagination and comprehension.

Picture books and chapter books for children ages 4 - 8 will work best for "What Happens Next?" As you begin, look for natural opportunities to stop and discuss. However, I recommend pausing for "What Happens Next?" only one to two times in a story. You risk losing interest and comprehension if you spend too much time outside the story. It's a delicate balance, to be certain! It may take some practice, so be patient with yourself and your child. But I bet you both will find this adds a delightful new dimension to your read-aloud moments.

Grow: Cliffhanger moments can spark questions and encourage curiosity from stories read aloud!

EEKK! A Not-So-Scary Approach to Reading Aloud

It's 6:10 p.m. You've just picked up your kids from soccer practice, and you're exhausted from the demanding day. You drop your keys on the counter only to hear the rumblings of your offspring chiming, "I'm hungry!" "When are we eating dinner?"

Without hesitation, you respond, "You two start on your homework while I start dinner." A quick response makes you feel efficient and on top of things. Until they both reply in stereo, "We finished it already!"

It's a worst-case scenario because even an express dinner of nuggets and steamed veggies is twenty minutes out. In a panic, all you can mutter is, "EEKK!" You don't want the TV on, and you don't want them on devices either, which adds to your dilemma. How will you keep them busy? What can they do for the next twenty minutes? After a quick pause, you remember they always have reading!

"While I get dinner ready, you can grab books for twenty minutes of 'EEKK' reading." They've done this before, so they know exactly what you're talking about and head off to grab books.

Keeping little ones engaged with an open book can be difficult, especially at home. Distractions are numerous when television, technology, music, people, and even pets clamor for attention.

But let's consider a simple and practical suggestion for families with more than one reader in the home: have your children read together as partners. It's a convenient solution with easy implementation. They can sit side by side, elbow to elbow, knee to knee—EEKK! Here is a fun little poem to remind them how to share a reading experience.

Elbow to elbow

Knee to knee

I read to you

You read to me

Elbow to elbow

Knee to knee

Book in the middle

So we both can see!

The idea is that each child will read the text on their side of the page and then listen as their partner, sibling, parent, etc., reads. Partner reading will work best by placing the book on the floor between them or having each one hold a side of the book to read and follow along. It's an effective way for readers to practice reading and listening, boosting their confidence and skills. It will be essential to choose a book that is at the appropriate level for both readers. Sometimes, the text is simple for one of them. But it's still a great way to keep siblings occupied while sharing a book, assuming your children get along well.

Suppose siblings aren't compatible with a shared reading experience. It can also work with a parent, caregiver, grandparent, or even during a playdate. The method is flexible and can be adapted to various situations, making it a valuable tool for engaging children in reading at home.

Set a blanket for reading, and kids can sit on pillows, read in a special area of the house, and bring in some stuffed animals to listen along. A little creativity goes a long way; the more often your kids read, the more words they will learn. And that's what we will talk about in the next chapter!

Grow: Partner reading allows two readers to practice reading and listening, boosting skills and confidence!

Two stories, Four words: Ill, Enormous, Conundrum, Crisp

Story One

One day, while at the library, my daughter was browsing books to purchase for her classroom while I read from a book of well-told tales to my grandson. The first story we read was *Little Red Riding Hood*. As you likely know, the story begins with Red heading to her grandmother's house to deliver a basket of treats because Grandma is ill. I paused on the page to inquire about the word ill. I said, "Do you know what the word ill means?" To which he replied with confidence, "Yes, it means sick." I was pleased and continued reading. A few pages later brought us to the story, *The Enormous Turnip*. I felt certain my grandson hadn't heard this story, but he was very engaged, so I started to read. Once again, the story began with a challenging vocabulary word. I asked, "Do you know what the word enormous means?" He replied with animation, "Yes, Gigi, it means really big!"

I nodded in agreement while astonished at the vocabulary knowledge of this three-year-old child. And then I remembered his experience with books as a toddler. One of his favorite stories was a board book titled: *Eek! Halloween!* by Sandra Boynton. He loved that book and would sit with it in his lap, reading and rereading his favorite part. After reciting "strange things are happening" in a sing-song voice, he would turn to the page where a mouse was "enormous." He would point to the mouse, look at his mama, and say "enormous" in his best almost two-year-old voice. And that's one way we begin sharing advanced vocabulary with our littles!

Story Two

I spent eighteen years teaching second grade, which brought me tons of joy and oodles of opportunities to teach literacy in many facets of my day. My seven-year-old students were often eager to learn and apply their newly acquired literacy skills. Generally, it was in the classroom, but this story happened one morning after recess. A few of my students, who happened to be best friends and who also happened to love roughhousing, had overdone it on the playground. What started as a friendly tussle became a fight with punches and bruises. Not being the first time this had occurred, my students returned to me "post-scuffle" with a note from the office and a note they had to write home. One note went something like this:

Dear Dad and Mom,

Today, during recess, my friends and I played and pushed each other. Someone pushed me too hard, and I had to punch back even though it was my friend. I was in trouble for hitting my friends last week, so this is a conundrum! I wrote an apology, and I will miss recess for the rest of the week.

Your Son

Did you catch that? Did you see CONUNDRUM?! My students and I had been discussing the word conundrum during class. We talked about how it was a problem that involved some confusion. Although I was disappointed that my student chose to hit his friend, I was thrilled he used the newly acquired vocabulary word correctly.

Exposure to higher level vocabulary does not have to involve a specific teaching technique. You can help your child acquire new words by substituting a more complex word for the one you commonly use. For example, instead of saying it's cold outside, try using the words chilly, freezing, cool, or crisp. In the context of many different situations, we can substitute words.

Let's imagine a scenario where your children have started arguing or fighting. (This is purely hypothetical, of course. I know your children don't do that!) You now have a chance to use the word mad. But you could make this a teaching moment and provide a synonym for emphasis such as angry, upset, furious, or outraged. Do you see where I'm going with this?

Often, just a bit of intentionality will help us create a learning opportunity!

82

Grow: Switching out one common word with a complex one can help advance your child's vocabulary.

Make It Count! STEM/STEAM

There has been a significant push for STEM and STEAM in education over the past two decades. These fields, including Science, Technology, Engineering, Mathematics, and the Arts, have seen a surge as individuals and groups work to develop and incorporate skills and strategies needed to prepare children for a world with innovative jobs and new technologies. As parents, grandparents, and caregivers, we can continue this momentum at home with an array of books to support.

What does that look like in a home library? So glad you asked!

Books with numbers, counting, and sets of items are excellent beginnings for the littlest. Nature, animals, and seasons can teach young ones about the world around them. Pull a few blocks, figurines, and toys to count along as you read. Or see if you can find a stuffed animal that matches the animal you're reading about that day.

Children are naturally curious, so it shouldn't take much to help your little ones engage with science, technology, engineering, math, and the arts. As a parent, you play a crucial role in this process as you provide the stories and encourage your littles to explore the world around them. If you show interest, your child will likely follow your lead. Choose books that make you wonder! Then, model your thinking and questioning as you read to your little one.

As your children become older, let's say ages 3-7, they will know what sparks their interest. You can capitalize on this excellent opportunity to allow them to select their books (with guidance, of course). Encourage them to choose a variety of stories. STEAM books will often include photographs and activities. You will find most of the books are nonfiction.

However, you may find a picture book blending fiction with nonfiction. One of my favorites is *Ada Twist, Scientist* by Andrea Beatty. Beatty masterfully combines rollicking rhyme and clever storytelling to engage the minds of young readers in her series, *The Questioneers,* inspired by real-life makers Ada Lovelace and Marie Curie.

When kids are ages 7 – 10, they can read and research on their own. You can offer suggestions and support as you uncover some fantastic STEM books. Facts, photos, and hands-on activities can enhance your at-home reading experiences. Have your child share a few newly acquired bits of information and then plan to try out an experiment or two. Weekends, school breaks, and summer vacation could be an opportune time to put this into practice!

Another way to use STEAM is to introduce biographies. Biographies detail facts and information about a particular individual and are a fantastic way for little ones to learn about the people behind the inventions and innovations. Read and research people who have made strides in the field of STEAM. Choose a figure and find out more! You may find biographies written by the same author. Your child might appreciate a favorite author's familiar writing style and pattern. An example is *Ordinary People Change the World Series* by Brad Meltzer, written for children ages 5-9 with kid-friendly illustrations, pertinent facts, and fun!

Grow: Highlight science, technology, engineering, math, and arts with books that tap into your child's intellect, innovation, and wonder.

Books and Coffee—A Book Date

A Saturday morning with no agenda spells particular delight as she scurries out with keys and purse in hand for a morning adventure. After a quick arrival at her destination, she opens the heavy glass door to be greeted by two enchanting smells—new books and coffee. After a deep inhale, she ambles back to the kids' section of the store. There, she spends a few minutes perusing the covers of the newest releases, each a potential treasure waiting to be discovered. It's all part of the thrill of finding a new book and the excitement of what the story might hold. She chooses a few and plops on the floor in bliss. Eventually, she chooses one and grabs a coffee before strolling to the checkout line. Her twenty-dollar adventure soothes her literary soul and adds to her collection of terrific titles for the classroom.

This book outing was a joy for the mama in this story, but did you know that kids enjoy book dates too? Children are often just as excited to add a new book to their home library, so include them in your book adventures. There is immense value in investing in a good book, and it's important to enjoy your experience too.

We can find books at numerous locations! Barnes & Noble is one place to find new releases, but many others exist. Have you ever checked out a local or indie bookstore? Target, Walmart, and Kohl's stores also sell new books. Many people buy books online at Amazon, Booksource.com, Christianbooks.com, Scholastic.com, and more. Have you considered books that have been gently used? Try Friends of the Library bookstore! You can also find previously owned books at thrift stores, secondhand stores, and garage sales.

There are countless ways to add to your child's library. Choose one today and create an adventure. Bring your favorite little reader along and make it a book date!

Grow: Take your child on a book date to choose a new or gently used title to add to your home library.

Wonder, Whimsy, Wishes

Wonder, whimsy, wishes

When we find wonder and whimsy in our world, we can create moments that extend the literature our littles read. Let's get creative and make reading fun! This section showcases ideas we can implement to enhance book experiences with our families. Here, we can take the wishes of our dandelion dreams and turn them into literacy legacies!

Baking and Books

When my daughters were little, we always celebrated holidays with extras—extra decorations, extra books, extra festivities, extra sweets! (We were "extra" before it was even a thing.) Inevitably, the sweets involved baking cookies, and sugar cookies were our go-to. It wasn't that we loved sugar cookies, although my youngest might disagree, but rather that I could roll out the dough and use shaped cutters to create small wonders of delight.

We made cookies often, but I was teaching full-time while raising my girls, so I went the convenient route and purchased premade cookie dough and tubs of white icing. We would roll out the dough on wax paper and then take turns using the holiday-themed cutters. I would place them on a cookie sheet for eleven to thirteen minutes at 350 degrees, and voilà, we had personal little canvases for decorating.

My oldest daughter loves frosting, so this was always her favorite part. I would create little color palettes that matched the holiday using small bowls and food coloring. We would deftly smooth the colored frosting onto each cookie with plastic knives. It was colorful but not very fancy until . . . the secret. When you decorate sugar cookies, you need sugars and sprinkles—lots of them because this is where you become fancy, festive, and fun. And if you want to kick it up a notch, purchase matching paper plates and napkins to serve them!

The sugar cookie tradition began when I was a little girl. My brother and I would bake them with my mom at Christmas. I loved it and continued the tradition when my girls were little but for almost every holiday. Now that I have a grandson, our tradition has a new twist. I buy a new book or several to read before or after making our cookies. We grab a book, snuggle up and read. I have affectionately coined it "Cookies and Cuddles."

Maybe reading this makes you feel a little stressed out. Life gets busy! It's hard to pause and enjoy the little things. But as a Gigi and former educator, let me gently remind you that those little things are your children, grandchildren, and maybe even great-grandchildren. They are precious, and they grow ever so quickly. Why not begin making memories and creating traditions that may carry on well beyond your lifetime? Take a moment to slow down, enjoy the process of baking cookies, and read books with your littles. You're invited to celebrate with our family cookie tradition, or perhaps you'll start your own. But be sure to pull in a book or two as you make new memories with your little ones.

Grow: Baking and reading books are fantastic ways to create new memories with your little ones!

Planes, Trains and Automobiles

When you think of summer vacation, what comes to mind? Road trip!

Picture this: an ambitious family sets out on a summer vacation road trip. Four adults and two children squeeze into a sedan for a 2,000-mile trek to Yellowstone National Park and back. It's a brave adventure but fantastic for the family. Numerous stops are made along the way, primarily at National Parks and lodges for a night's rest. There is no radio on in the car as the group's oldest members aren't keen on the current rock and pop music. Without iPads or iPhones, what do they do to pass the time? They talk and read (those who don't get carsick). Snuggled up in the backseat, one of the little ones passes the time with an activity book. It's jampacked with word searches, crossword puzzles, rebus puzzles, dot-to-dots, and mazes. She's occupied for hours.

So, does an activity book count as an actual book? It doesn't have many words; it doesn't tell a story. There isn't a setting, characters, problem, or solution. Does this count as summer reading?

Activity books engage the brain! They require attention and focus, as well as the manipulation of words in different ways. Thinking skills, problem-solving, and creativity are all checkpoints with an activity book. But best of all, activity books are portable and make a great diversion on a road trip, flight, airport waiting, or train ride. Did you know that many beloved children's books have online printables that showcase a character in combination with activities? And best of all, activity books are fun!

We need to plan when we think of traveling by plane, train, or automobile. We decide what to wear according to our destination and what to bring to maximize our fun, especially if it's a vacation. What would it look like to consider traveling with book fun for our kiddos? Let's choose a few new titles to bring along. Or better yet, let them select a couple of new books! Look for an activity book, online printables, or download an audiobook for the family. When we can make reading fun, we will grow young readers, one book and activity book at a time!

Grow: Take books and activity books when you travel to keep littles reading and make reading fun!

Sharing is Caring!

One of the key components of raising little ones is teaching them how to be a good human. We value words like "please and thank you," so we start early with our instruction. When our children ask for something, we teach them to say "please." When we give it to them, we teach them to reply with "thank you" as they receive it. Sharing is another concept we hold in high regard. Parents spend a great deal of time teaching their little ones the value of sharing, not just a social skill but a responsibility. It's fascinating that children innately speak "no" and "mine" without much prompting. Teaching our kids to share can take patience and time, but the reward is worth the effort. We want children to be considerate and kind, so we teach them the importance of sharing their things. Often, it's toys, but books should fall into the category of things we can share with others.

Book Exchanges

Perhaps your children have grown tired of some of the stories living in your home and could be enjoyed by neighborhood kids.

Why not host a neighborhood book exchange? Book exchanges promote sharing and kindness and enhance reading experiences. Choose a day and time for the exchange, put out a table for the available titles, allow browsing with eyes first, and then a systematic approach to selecting a "new to you" book to take home.

Another suggestion is to book trade with another family or group of friends. If you want the book returned, I recommend placing a sticker, label, or nameplate on it. A book log would be a great way to keep track of books out on loan. Trading books monthly, quarterly, or bi-annually will allow your child to share books and enjoy new titles.

Bookie Cookie Exchange

Holidays are a perfect time to emphasize giving, caring, and sharing. December creates an opportunity to include our children with festivities and kindness toward others. Host a "Bookie Cookie Exchange" for your kiddos. This idea is in the tradition of good old adult cookie exchanges in which you bring a set number of cookies to a party and then leave with a sampling of different cookies to take home. However, in the Bookie Cookie Exchange, each child brings a new book to donate to a family in need, a book for trading, and a dozen cookies to share. Parents can collect the new books and find a charitable organization accepting and distributing donations. Adults can also help facilitate the cookie sharing and sampling. Kiddos select a book from the book trade table and enjoy a "new to you" book and some fun holiday treats!

Books at a Discount

Purchasing books can be an investment in reading but also an expense. For some, the affordability of books could be a deterrent to purchases. To assist you with more affordable places to buy books, I've compiled a short list of resources for places to find books at a discounted price.

- <u>Friends of the Library:</u> Many public libraries have attached bookstores, selling gently used titles at ridiculously low prices.

- <u>Thrift stores:</u> You may need to visit thrift stores often, and as you gather, be sure you're thorough in your selections. While it takes a bit of time, flipping through the book before you purchase will ensure the pages aren't damaged.

- <u>Garage sales:</u> Have some free time on a Saturday morning? Check out your local garage sales for some gently used literary treasures!

Short on time? Keep reading for four online shopping possibilities.

Scholastic.com is a site that offers new book sets and new individual books at a significantly discounted price. The "parent" tab allows you to select an age range or topic of interest. You can go from there! A few more suggestions include: Thriftbooks.com, Bookoutlet.com, and Abebooks.com. Remember that some sites sell new books, and others sell preowned ones, so research before purchasing.

Grow: Book exchanges are an inexpensive way to give and receive new book titles, and purchasing gently owned books can build your home library at an affordable price.

When Kids Love Reading, Everyone Can Cheer!

Imagine a cozy fire, a warm cup of cocoa, and the newest release from a favorite author. Everyone gathers with expectation as the first person leads the conversation, sharing key takeaways and asking questions. One at a time, each member takes a turn to weigh in or add to the conversation. This framework is one for a book club meeting. Does this sound familiar? Have you been to a book club meeting? If adults find book clubs rewarding, would it work for children?

Let's face it: some kids love reading, and some don't. We understand the challenge of sparking children's interest in reading. But what if we could change that? What if there was a way for the whole family to enjoy reading? Try implementing a Mama and Me Book Club, Families and Fiction Book Club, or Grandparents and Great Titles Book Club!

Of course, choosing a book will be the first step, but there are a few more considerations. You'll want to:

- Collaborate: include your child in decisions such as what to read, when to meet, pages or chapters to read before meeting, and a special treat for snacks

- <u>Carve out time:</u> daily reading of the book of choice and monthly meetings

- <u>Conversations:</u> discuss elements of the book such as plot, conflict, resolution, illustrations, setting, favorite characters, favorite sections, chapters read, or an alternative ending

- <u>Celebrate:</u> pages read, book completion, and accomplishments along the way

- <u>Create a calendar:</u> institute a year-long focus for the reading your book club will include. Here are suggestions to get you started:

> January - new beginnings
>
> February - friendships
>
> March - nonfiction
>
> April - poetry
>
> May - heroes
>
> June - fairytales
>
> July - biography
>
> August - celebrating success
>
> September - fiction
>
> October - science
>
> November - gratitude
>
> December - book from a favorite series

Everyone has a role in this activity, which invites opportunities for literacy to expand beyond the daily routines you encourage in your household. So add a little spice and give a book club a try!

100

Grow: Celebrate books in a shared literacy experience with a monthly meetup in a family book club.

Author's Chair

Literacy routines are essential for elementary aged children. Routines help ensure that each language arts section is addressed (taught) and completed (learned). Language arts consist of reading, writing, speaking, listening, and language. Many states, school districts, and educational institutions adhere to "standards-based" instruction, which provides the expected outcomes of what will be taught and learned. In addition, an established curriculum assesses mastery of skills and includes remediation. There are various implementation models beyond the expectations and guides accompanying language arts instruction. These models suggest ways to implement curriculum and activities to support learning.

My teaching experience took place in a traditional classroom setting. Over twenty-three years, I implemented numerous language arts programs and reading models. However, one model was my favorite because it was student-centered. I taught and assessed all the required curriculum, but I provided my students with choices in many activities. For example, during our language arts block, the children had five areas of literacy to complete, but they could choose the order in which to complete them and where to sit in the classroom. I loved this literacy model, and the students did too!

One of the highlights for my students and me was "Author's Chair." This activity fostered writing skills while encouraging creative self-expression. During independent writing time, students could write books. Using blank 8x11 inch copy paper folded in half and stapled, a bin of blank books was waiting for stories. Student authors could write about various topics, including make-believe stories, facts about something they knew and enjoyed, or an alternative ending to a favorite book they read. A student would often work to write their book in a week and use "fast finisher" time for the illustrations. When the book was complete, they read it to a friend and then put their name on the whiteboard list to share during "Author's Chair" time. Sitting in my teacher's chair, the author read aloud to the class, and after, we would give positive feedback to the writer. "Author's Chair" culminated in reading, writing, speaking, listening, and language; we all loved it!

There is a great sense of accomplishment in producing your own written work and great value in reading it aloud to someone. While I used "Author's Chair" in a traditional classroom, it can be just as effective in a homeschool setting and at home. If you're homeschooling, perhaps you'd like to build this into your literacy routine. When we find ways to incorporate reading, writing, listening, and speaking, we extend the experience with books. So why not let your child try this? You can give your child the opportunity to be an author on the weekend, during school breaks, or during summer vacations.

Grow: Activities such as "Author's Chair" combine multiple elements of language arts and allow children to share their creative work with others!

Books and Reels

It can be challenging to keep children "hooked" on reading for pleasure as they age. Many activities, sports, school obligations, technology, and friends will fight for their attention. They want to be independent and often don't want to be bothered by your insistence on keeping tabs with their literacy growth. While we want to foster independence, it is still imperative that you know when and what your child is reading.

Understanding your child's reading choices can help you guide them toward more enriching and age-appropriate content. There is tremendous literature for school-age children, but the opposite is also true. You can use a resource such as CommonSense.org to check Lexile levels and age appropriateness for books.

Once you have a handle on the books your child is reading, see if you can help them carry a literacy experience into the theater. Perhaps a book has been made into a movie or will be a coming attraction. Buy and read the book together, or have your child read it first and tell you about it. Then, plan to see the movie when it comes out or watch it at home. You could arrange a family date night or a parent/child outing. And be sure to discuss what was the same and different about the book and the movie. Here are some sample discussion questions to consider:

- Which one was better?

- Would you recommend it to a friend? Why or why not?

- If nonfiction, could it have been made as a fictional book/movie? How so?

- If it was fiction, could it have been made a nonfiction book/movie? How so?

Here are some books that have become movies:

A Wrinkle in Time
Polar Express
Cloudy with a Chance of Meatballs
The Cat in the Hat
The Grinch
Charlotte's Web
Charlie and the Chocolate Factory
Chronicles of Narnia
Harry Potter Series
The Secret Garden
Matilda
Little Women
Where the Wild Things Are
How to Train Your Dragon

Wizard of Oz
The Jungle Book
Classic Disney Fairy Tales
A Series of Unfortunate Events
Percy Jackson
Wonder

Of course, you will want to choose books and movies that align with your child's interests and your family values. But books and movies can be a fun way to extend stories into weekend fun!

Grow: Movies can be a fun culmination or incentive for reading a book first!

That Stuck with Me

Sticky notes, those delightful little tools, can bring a burst of color and assistance while reading. They are available in different sizes and hues and can be a valuable asset to reading. How, you may wonder? Allow me to enlighten you!

Let's say your child reads a chapter book and comes across an unfamiliar word. There are several options at this point:

1. Stop reading and ask a parent for the definition.

2. Stop reading and look up the word online or in a dictionary.

3. Skip the word entirely and continue reading (hoping to use context clues to figure out what the word means).

4. Write the word on a sticky note and return to it at the end of the page or chapter.

Numbers three and four together are my recommendations for implementing the use of sticky notes for new vocabulary. Often, a reader can gain context from the surrounding sentences of the story. Perhaps enough to maintain comprehension and keep the fluency of the text. If so, a sticky note can be a handy marker for the reader. At the end of the page or even the chapter, the child can return to the challenging new word and look up the definition. Rereading the sentence should clarify and add a new word to the reader's vocabulary.

Another use of sticky notes is to jot down a question, observation, thought, or concern that may emerge while reading a story. Again, the sticky note serves as a placeholder and reminder for the reader to revisit the story without interrupting its flow.

Sticky notes are perfect for recording notes about a favorite part of the story or predicting what may happen next. And for parents who want to add an element of surprise, leaving a sticky note in an unread book can create a delightful moment of anticipation as your child reads.

Grow: Sticky notes can be a fabulous tool for bookmarking pages and writing down unknown words to look up during or after reading.

Wish You Were Here—Reading Postcards

It was August 1978 when a quick trip to the mailbox offered a colorful surprise. A small 4x6 card held a conglomeration of photos depicting this location's beauty. Examining the card closely, one could read the scripted font that detailed the precise landmark and location of these photos. On the back, a greeting from a loved one or friend who had been visiting. Only a few words fit in the small space, and then a quick signature followed by *P.S. Wish you were here!*

Postcards were all the rage back in the 60s, 70s, and 80s! You can still find them today when you travel. They live on a circular metal display in touristy souvenir stores. And while most of us don't spend the time to mail out a postcard to friends and family from our vacation destinations (thank you, interwebs), this postcard idea is great for a reading/writing extension.

If you have a not-so-little reader, try this! After reading a favorite picture book, invite your child to create a postcard. You'll need a blank 3x5 or 4x6 index card. On one side, your child draws a picture that depicts the story's setting (the setting is where the story takes place). It could be a scene from the story or simply the location. On the back side, they write a short note from the main character to another or from the main character to someone real or imaginary.

What does this look like? Below are a few examples.

Let's say you've just read *The Lorax* by Dr. Seuss. On one side, your child can draw a scene from the story. Perhaps the page with the factory and the chopped-down Truffula trees. On the back side, a short note like this:

> *Dear Once-ler Family,*
>
> *We need you to stop chopping down our Truffula trees. The Bar-ba-loots are hungry, and the Swamee-swans have left. Please help restore this place so that others can enjoy it!*
>
> *Regards,*
> *The Lorax*

Here's another example from *Duck and Goose: Honk! Quack! Boo!* by Tad Hills. Your child can draw a scene with Duck and Goose dressed up in costume, ready to trick-or-treat.

> *Hi Friends!*
>
> *Grab your costume and meet us in the forest for a fun night of trick-or-treating. We hope to see you there!*
>
> *Your Friends,*
> *Duck and Goose*

One final example is *Cheetahs*, a nonfiction Level 2 reader from National Geographic Kids. Children can address this postcard to a parent, grandparent, friend, etc., using facts about cheetahs and writing questions. On the back side, include a picture of a cheetah in the savanna.

Dear Gigi,

I'm enjoying the savanna in Africa. Can you guess what I have seen here? Cheetahs! They have cool spots, and you should see how fast they run! Did you know that cheetahs are the fastest land animals on earth? Wish you were here!

Love,
Sara

Of course, these are just a few ways to extend a story with your kids. Encourage them to add creative details and spend quality time with writing and drawing. Postcards work well as an individual project but could also be a partner activity. The possibilities are endless!

Grow: Writing postcards is a creative way to extend reading. This enjoyable activity combines drawing, recall, story elements, and art!

Let's Have a Little Fun

Children thrive on fun; we can inspire good literacy habits by making reading fun! Below you'll see some creative ideas for infusing fun into reading. Practically speaking, this won't be a daily or even weekly experience. But weekends, summer vacations, and breaks from school are perfect times to participate in some fun literacy adventures. And if you need a few suggestions, keep reading!

Mix it Up – Books and Baking

Kids in the kitchen might sound daunting, but with a bit of planning and prepping, you can make a moment a memory with books and baking! First up, "Cookies and Cuddles." Baking with little ones is referenced in the chapter "Baking and Books." You will find a thorough description of creating baking moments and memories with your children.

However, this chapter will focus on "Cookies and Cuddles." So, once you pop your cookies (whichever recipe you enjoy) into the oven, you and your little one can cuddle up with a favorite book while your cookies are baking. Time spent with books will make the cookie baking and eating a little sweeter! If you have more time, try baking a cake for "Cake and Cuddles."

Are you looking for a breakfast treat? Give "Muffins and Memories" a try. If you are a baking connoisseur, you might make your sweet treats from scratch, but boxed goods and packaged refrigerated cookie dough work well too! Pulling in a book as part of your baking experience is the most important thing. And if you're looking for clever ideas for combining books and bites, take a peek below!

- Bake and take picnic - pack some favorite books and have a picnic lunch

- *Pinkalicious* - bake up some fun with a pink cupcake party

- *Nate the Great* - have a pancake breakfast like the characters in the story

- Laura Numeroff's books - *If You Give a Mouse a Cookie, If You Give a Dog a Donut, If You Give a Moose a Muffin, If You Give a Pig a Pancake*

- *Dragons Love Tacos* - gather up all the goodies and have a taco party

- Patricia Polacco's *Thundercake* - bake a "thundercake" (recipe included in the book) and extra credit for the not-so-littles when you have them write about fears

- *The Very Hungry Caterpillar* -take a field trip to the farmer's market or grocery store and pick up some of the healthy foods that the caterpillar eats

Baking might not be your thing, no problem! Keep reading for alternative suggestions to keep fun in the equation as you create moments and memories. Why not consider:

Paper Bag Puppets

If you have some brown paper bags, construction paper, glue sticks, and markers, you have the supplies to make paper bag puppets. Kids can create a character from a fictional story using the craft supplies. Important tip: the bottom of the bag becomes the face, so when your child puts their hand into the bag, they can move it up and down to act out the story.

On the Go

I'm a big fan of books on the go! You can take books along for fun or purchase them when you're out exploring places like field trips to the library, friends of the library, concert in the park, zoo or wildlife center, the aquarium, or museum!

Themes

Choosing themes for book selections can create an interest and focus for your reading. You could select one a week or one each month—anything that brings a smile and some excitement to your literacy moments. Here are a few to get you started: animals, holidays, seasons, characters, or genres such as poetry, nonfiction, fantasy, or sci-fi.

Camp Out/Camp In

Set up a tent, grab a blanket, flashlight, and some favorite books for an outdoor or indoor adventure. Want to kick it up a notch? Try some indoor s'mores!

October Delights

Paint and/or decorate a pumpkin like a book character. This activity is sure to inspire creativity and delight.

Fairy Tale Fun

Pick one a week—original, fractured, or one from another country and compare the similarities and differences among these stories.

Grow: Weekends, holidays, school breaks, and summer vacations are great times to introduce creative activities that support literacy in your home!

Getting Grandparents Involved

Wednesday nights are FaceTime Read-Alouds with Gigi. I call my grandson and read him a story on FaceTime with my laptop! It's a great way to stay connected midweek since I usually don't see him. And it's also a delightful way for us to share a story!

One week, however, I had the joy of picking up my little guy at school, so our read-aloud happened in person during our donut date. My book choice was *If You Give a Dog a Donut* by Laura Numeroff and Felicia Bond. I LOVE the "If You Give" series, and this one takes the cake—well, DONUT! It's always fun pairing a book and a treat, so this combo was terrific.

Beyond the fun, grandparents have a unique opportunity to impact literacy for little ones. A weekly read-aloud can instill a love for reading and learning in our grandchildren. And since almost everyone owns a cellphone or laptop, it is a special treat. You might wonder what this looks like for children of different ages. I'll share a few examples with you.

One of my friends has a nine-month-old grandson whom she reads with weekly on a FaceTime call. His mama holds the phone, and my friend holds the book as she reads and turns the pages. Of course, he is too little to focus the entire time, but it is still a deep connection they are making as he listens to her voice. Another friend of mine has grandchildren of elementary age. She jumps on Zoom each month to have a "book club" meetup with them, and they discuss the chapters they have read. What a fantastic way to stay connected with her grandchildren!

Grandparents can play a special role in the lives of our littles. They offer endless hugs and lavish loads of love and often spoil our little ones with gifts. Time spent with grandparents can nurture and grow a bond that extends beyond our role as parents. When we encourage grandparents to participate in shared literacy experiences, we tap into a resource that deepens a connection with our children.

Book dates with grandparents are a creative way to combine time and literacy. Whether in-person or by phone, book dates keep generations connected with fun. And if grandparents are eager to purchase gifts, why not suggest a book? Making memories with grandkids over a midweek read-aloud is as simple as a phone call and a story. These shared experiences will create lasting memories that will be cherished by grandparents and grandkids alike!

Grow: Grandparents can participate in a shared literacy experience with a FaceTime read-aloud or in-person book date!

I Wish

If I could go back and tell my twenty-two-year-old self, something about growing little readers, it would be this:

- Read every day.

- Have several books to choose from.

- Trade books with friends.

- Buy books from Friends of the Library.

- Ask for books as gifts.

- Give books to your friends when they have babies.

- Interact with your little readers.

- Let your kids bring books everywhere.

- Make reading fun.

I wish I had known how important a solid foundation in literacy is for children under the age of six. I wish I had played more phonemic awareness games with my oldest daughter. I wish I had started a family read-aloud tradition when my daughters were young. I wish I had read for leisure more when they were elementary aged so they would see me model my love of reading.

Hindsight is 20/20! I can't turn back the hands of time, but I can help encourage parents now! That is my hope for this book. You can start building a love of literacy for your little ones in many ways. And you can start today! If you commit to reading for ten to fifteen minutes each day, you help establish a foundation for reading that can be long-lasting. Your time and commitment now will benefit your child for years to come, paving the way for a lifelong love of reading.

While I can't change the past, I'm grateful for the many things I did right when reading to my girls. We shared countless moments of joy and bonding over books. As I learned about literacy as a teacher, I was able to implement good practices at home to encourage reading in the elementary years. My daughters have grown to be solid readers with strong literacy skills, and they use them daily as teachers. And now that I have a grandson, I've had a second chance at pulling in all the tips and tools I've gathered.

So here is my current wish list:

I wish for you and your child to love reading. I want every child, regardless of their circumstances, to have a personal library with at least twenty books. I wish children would build experiences with books that keep them engaged and reading daily. Most of all, I wish each child would become a solid reader with a heart for books and a love of literacy!

Will you join me in helping to make these wishes come true?

ACKNOWLEDGEMENTS

First and foremost, I thank God for the dream he placed in my heart to write a literacy guide for families so that littles may grow to love reading. He's been with me throughout each page of this book, and I'm grateful!

Michael, you have been patient and encouraging with all my creative endeavors over the past five years (and we both know there's been a lot). You've supported me financially and believed in my dreams; you always say yes! Even when you have no idea what I'm doing, you make space for me to work and nudge me forward when I get distracted. Thirty-six years of loving you – you have my heart!

Brianna and Nicole, this book was born from the joy I experienced reading with both of you as babies, toddlers, and elementary-aged kiddos. Our shared memories of reading together have been a source of inspiration for my words. We learned the value of investing in children at home and school together. As teachers, you put this into practice daily. I'm forever grateful for your listening ears and constructive critique throughout this book. My heart bursts when I think of how blessed I am to be your mama!

Cortez, my precious grandson! You are the subject of so many chapters in this book. I will forever treasure the giggles and joy we shared and continue to share while discovering that books and creative play extend the love of reading. May you always love books, and may you always know that Gigi loves you more than you can even imagine!

Dad, you've always believed I could do anything! Quick to encourage and boost my confidence with your kind and careful words, you continue to support my wildly creative dreams. I know my love of education and words has trickled down from you. I love you!

Jeff, my website designer, headshot photographer, and patient responder to all my tech questions, thank you for sharing my excitement for this journey! From childhood, as a brother/sister creative team, we have stuck together like Snoopy and Woodstock, always there for each other and ready to support in any way we can. Love ya!

Stephanie, president of my fan club, like my little sister and longest friend, your contagious enthusiasm for my projects is unmatched. You are one of the first to celebrate and want to shout from the rooftops. Words cannot express how grateful I am for your support each step of the way. You are precious to me!

Sweet Sara, thank you for teaching me to pay attention to the little things! We hold a special place in our hearts for teaching

Kinders; I'm grateful for the years I observed your skill and finesse as I taught alongside you in K and 2nd grade. Our travels, chats, and cherished memories will forever fill my heart!

To my extended family and friends (with a special shout out to Lil, Debby, Bunkey, and Patty), your unwavering support has been a cornerstone of this journey. Thank you for always listening to my many words, subscribing to my newsletters, and cheering me on along the way! I have felt your prayers and your support, and I'm thankful.

Laurie, our friendship began in high school and blossomed as we attended college together and became mamas. I am richly blessed to have your love, encouragement, and support as we journey through life's lows and highs. Our creative connections and endeavors make me smile. Always just a phone call away, you fill my heart. Thank you, sweet friend!

Diana, you have helped me fund this project with generous donations to my Poshmark cause. Little by little, I took clothing and turned it into payment for coaching and writing fees. And I love that you implement recommendations from my book with your little ones. You are a gift!

Leslie, my long-distance writing comrade, and dear, sweet friend, you have been a constant source of encouragement and a prayer warrior for me. You've invited me to collaborate, been a Beta reader, and shared in this wonky writing world through lengthy phone conversations. Your authenticity and kindness inspire me. I adore you!

To my nonfiction writing gang, heaps of gratitude to each of you for listening, offering advice, and praying for this book. I value the support you have given me! I know it takes a village to bring a book into the world; thank you for being part of that village!

Bob Goff, Kimberly Stuart, Jessye, Harmony, Missy, Bayle, Beth, Claire, Lindsey, all my friends at The Oaks Conference Center, and each person I've met at Writer's Workshops and the Made for More retreat at The Oaks, you have blessed me in ways you may not know. Each kind word, gentle smile, reassuring hug, and cheering along the way brings a smile to my face. Y'all are inspirational, and you live life as trailblazers — love it!

To all my teacher and support staff friends, you know who you are, and too numerous to count! Thank you for the ways you touched my heart, even when you didn't know it! For hallway conversations, meet-ups in the pod, lunchtime lounge brainstorming, and collaboration. Your fortitude and commitment to the teaching profession is unwavering. I'm honored to have worked with each of you!

Mikaela, you have been my writing coach, editor, and patient teacher. This journey began over two years ago, and now we are here! We've spent countless hours on Zoom as you've coached me. I've cried, and we've laughed. I've asked thousands of questions, and you've provided answers. We've poured over editing, and we've celebrated each milestone. You say, "God loves to steer a moving ship," I agree wholeheartedly. Thank you for being "on board" with me!

To my cover image artist, Steve Bjorkman, for bringing a beautiful image of children celebrating their growth as readers to life! You are immensely talented, and I'm so thankful for your creativity, masterful skill, and collaboration on the cover design of this book. Your gift blesses many, my friend!

IBWAB Book Launch Team - you are the best! I'm so thankful for the joy and energy you brought to this experience. What a blessing it's been to have you by my side! So many thanks!

And to you, dear reader! Thank you for your investment in the gift of literacy for your littles. May they grow to love books and share that love with others. May they know that literacy is a gift, and it begins with a book!

END NOTES

Chapter 3:

1 Edutopia Brain-based Learning "Why Ages 2 - 7 Matter So Much for Brain Development" by Rishi Sriram June 24, 2020.

2 Perry Klass, M.D. FAAP, Anna Miller-Fitzwater, MD, MPH, FAAP, Pamela C. High, MD, MS, FAAP, COUNCIL ON EARLY CHILDHOOD

PEDIATRICS Volume 154, number 6, December 2024:e2024069090

To Cite: Klass P, Miller-Fitzwater A, High PC, et al; American Academy of Pediatrics, Council on Early Childhood. Literacy Promotion: An Essential Component of Primary Care Pediatric Practice: Policy Statement. Pediatrics. 2024;154(6): e2024069090

3 Child Mind Institute "Why Is It Important to Read to Your Child?" writer Hannah Sheldon-Dean, clinical expert Laura Phillips, PsyD ABPdN - the article was last reviewed or updated on December 2, 2024.

Chapter 15:

1 Giraffes, National Geographic Kids Readers Level 1, author Laura Marsh, pb. 2016

Get Started Early References

Brown, Margaret, and Clement Hurd. 1991. Goodnight Moon. New York: Harperfestival.

Dewdney, Anna. 2005. Llama Llama Red Pajama. Solon, Ohio: Findaway World, LLC.

Margaret Wise Brown, and Clement Hurd. 2017. The Runaway Bunny. New York, Ny: Harperfestival, An Imprint Of Harpercollinspublishers.

Martin, Bill, and Eric Carle. 1967. Brown Bear, Brown Bear, What Do You See? New York: Henry Holt and Company.

Schertle, Alice, and Jill Mcelmurry. 2016. Little Blue Truck. London: Nosy Crow.

Shaw, Nancy, and Margot Apple. 2016. Sheep in a Jeep. Boston, Massachusetts: Houghton Mifflin Harcourt.

Watt, Fiona. 2017. That's Not My Reindeer...

Read, Read, Read References

Baker, Keith. 2010. LMNO Peas. Simon and Schuster.

Boynton, Sandra. 1995. A to Z. New York, N.Y.: Little Simon Books, An Imprint Of Simon & Schuster Children's Publishing Division.

Carle, Eric. 2016. The Very Hungry Caterpillar's ABC Book. New York, New York: Grosset & Dunlap, An Imprint Of Penguin Random House Llc.

Ehlert L. 1993. Eating the Alphabet. Turtleback Books.

Giles Andreae, and Guy Parker-Rees. 2019. Giraffes Can't Dance. New York: Scholastic Inc.

Hegarty, Patricia. 2019. ABCs of Kindness. Random House Children's Books.

Kann, Victoria, and Elizabeth Kann. 2015. Pinkalicious. London: Hodder Children's Books, A Division Of Hachette Children's Books.

Kathleen Weidner Zoehfeld. 2018. Dinosaurs. Lerner Publishing Group.

Kontis, Alethea. 2012. AlphaOops! National Geographic Books.

Marsh, Laura. 2016. Giraffes. National Geographic Books.

Martin, Bill, and John Archambault. 1989. Chicka Chicka Boom Boom. S.L.: Simon & Schuster Books.

O'connor, Jane, Robin Preiss-Glasser, and Carolyn Bracken. 2009. Fancy Nancy. Heart to Heart. New York: Scholastic Inc.

Priddy, Roger. 2018. Alphaprints: ABC. Priddy Books US.

Seuss, Dr. 1991. Abc. New York: Random House, Inc.

Sherri Duskey Rinker. 2019. Cement Mixer's ABC. Chronicle Books.

Wood, Audrey, and Bruce Robert Wood. 2011. Alphabet Mystery. United States: Hatch.

Yolen, Jane, Mark Teague, and Findaway World, Llc. 2019. How Do Dinosaurs Say Good Night? Solon, Ohio: Findaway World, Llc.

Optimize Opportunities References

Beaty, Andrea. 2016. Ada Twist, Scientist. Abrams.

Boynton, Sandra. 2016. Eek! Halloween! Workman Publishing.

Dewdney, Anna. 2020. Llama Llama Misses Mama. New York, New York: Viking, An Imprint Of Penguin Young Readers Group.

John, Jory. 2021. Bad Seed. S.L.: Harperfestival.

John, Jory, and Pete Oswald. 2019. The Good Egg. New York, Ny: Harper, An Imprint Of Harpercollinspublishers.

Little. 1973. Little Red Riding Hood. London: Kaye & Ward.

Meltzer, Brad. 2020. Ordinary People Change the World: 22-Book Set. National Geographic Books.

Nietert, Michelle, and Tama Fortner. 2023a. God, I Feel Sad. Zonderkidz.

———. 2023b. God, I Feel Scared. Zonderkidz.

Penn, Audrey. 2018. The Kissing Hand. Indianapolis: Tanglewood.

Seuss, Dr. (1960) 2016. Green Eggs and Ham. London Harpercollins Children's Books.

———. (1957) 2017. The Cat in the Hat. London Harpercollins Children's Books.

Wheeler, Chris Andrew, and Lindsey Erin Wheeler. 2024. Kit and the Missing Notebook. Zonderkidz.

White, E. B. 1952. Charlotte's Web. New York, Ny: Harper, An Imprint Of Harpercollins Publishers.

Yates, Irene, and Jan Lewis. 1999. The Enormous Turnip. Ladybird Books.

Wonder, Whimsy, Wishes References

Carle, Eric. 1969. The Very Hungry Caterpillar. New York: Philomel Books.

Hills, Tad. 2017. Duck & Goose, Honk! Quack! Boo! Schwartz & Wade.

Kann, Victoria, and Elizabeth Kann. 2015. Pinkalicious. London: Hodder Children's Books, A Division Of Hachette Children's Books.

Laura Joffe Numeroff. 2015. If You Give a Mouse a Cookie. New York: Laura Geringer Book, An Imprint Of Harpercollins Publishers.

Laura Joffe Numeroff, and Felicia Bond. 2015. If You Give a Dog a Donut. New York: Harpercollins.

Laura Joffe Numeroff, Felicia Bond, and Kohl's Cares (Firm. 2015. If You Give a Pig a Pancake. New York: Laura Geringer Book, An Imprint Of Harper Collins Publishers.

Marjorie Weinman Sharmat. 2013. Nate the Great. Delacorte Press.

Marsh, Laura. 2018. Cheetahs. Lerner Publishing Group.

Numeroff, Laura Joffe, and Felicia Bond. 2022. If You Give a Moose a Muffin. New York: Balzer + Bray.

Polacco, Patricia. 1990. Thunder Cake. New York: Putnam & Grosset.

Rubin, Adam. 2013. Dragons Love Tacos. New York, Ny: Scholastic Inc.

Seuss, Dr. 1971. The Lorax. London: Harpercollins Children's Books.

AUTHOR CHRISTY SMITH

Connect with Christy

Christy Smith is a former educator with 23 years of classroom experience and a relentless passion for literacy. She delights in sharing ways to incorporate books into everyday life and create home environments where literacy can thrive. Living in sunny Orange County, California, Christy enjoys spending time with family and friends, savoring dark chocolate, and taking walks at Crystal Cove Beach.

You can find her engaged with mamas, sharing insights on social media, or her monthly newsletter at christiannewrites. com. Her heart for littles and literacy is profound; she believes every child deserves to love reading. And if you want to know the secret, *It Begins with a Book.*

Connect with Christy on Instagram: @christianne52619 or her website: @christiannewrites.com

COVER IMAGE ARTIST: STEVE BJORKMAN

Meet Steve

Steve Bjorkman has been fascinated with drawing since child-hood but has been able to make a living at it as an illustrator of picture books, greeting cards, ads, and magazines. A keen observer and constant sketcher of people and places, he has a special place in his heart for kids and reading.

www.ingramcontent.com/pod-product-compliance
Lightning Source LLC
Chambersburg PA
CBHW072237150726
48002CB00005B/2138